KU-026-132

BULLETPOINTS

HUMAN BODY

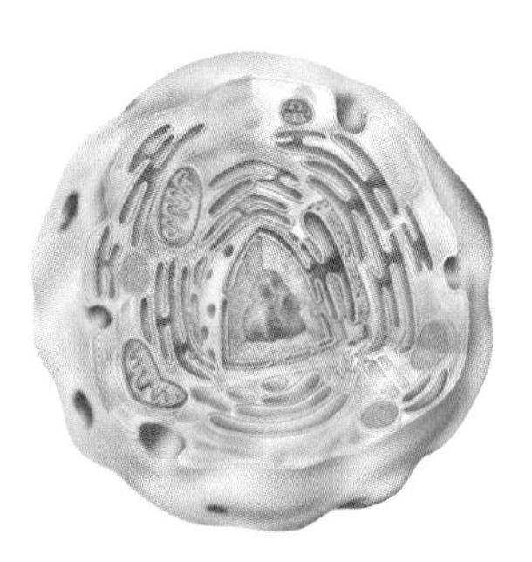

John Farndon
Consultant: Steve Parker

First published in 2003 by Miles Kelly Publishing Ltd
Bardfield Centre, Great Bardfield
Essex, CM7 4SL

Some material in this book first appeared in *1000 Things you should know*

2 4 6 8 10 9 7 5 3 1

Project Manager: Ruthie Boardman

Design: WhiteLight

Assistant: Carol Danenbergs

Production: Estela Godoy

British Library Cataloguing-in-Publication Data
A catalogue record for this book is available from the British Library

ISBN 1-84236-262-3

Printed in China

www.mileskelly.net
info@mileskelly.net

The publishers would like to thank the following artists who have contributed to this book:
Peter Gregory, Rob Jakeway, Janos Marffy, Annabel Milne, Tracy Morgan, Terry Riley, Mike Saunders, Rudi Vizi
All other pictures are from: MKP archives; Corel; DigitalSTOCK; digitalvision; PhotoDisc

Contents

Cells

- **Cells** are the basic building blocks of your body. Most are so tiny you would need 10,000 to cover a pinhead.
- **There are over 200 different kinds** of cell in your body, including nerve cells, skin cells, blood cells, bone cells, fat cells, muscle cells and many more.
- **A cell is basically** a little parcel of organic (life) chemicals with a thin membrane (casing) of protein and fat. The membrane holds the cell together, but lets nutrients in and waste out.
- **Inside the cell** is a liquid called cytoplasm, and floating in this are various minute structures called organelles.
- **At the centre** of the cell is the nucleus – this is the cell's control centre and it contains the amazing molecule DNA (see genes). DNA not only has all the instructions the cell needs to function, but also has the pattern for new human life.
- **Each cell** is a dynamic chemical factory, and the cell's team of organelles is continually busy – ferrying chemicals to and fro, breaking up unwanted chemicals, and putting together new ones.
- **The biggest cells** in the body can be nerve cells. Although the main nucleus of nerve cells is microscopic, the tails of some cells can extend for a metre or more through the body, and be seen even without a microscope.
- **Among the smallest cells** in the body are red blood cells. These are just 0.0075 mm across and have no nucleus, since nearly their only task is ferrying oxygen.
- **Most body cells** live a very short time and are continually being replaced by new ones. The main exceptions are nerve cells – these are long-lived, but rarely replaced.

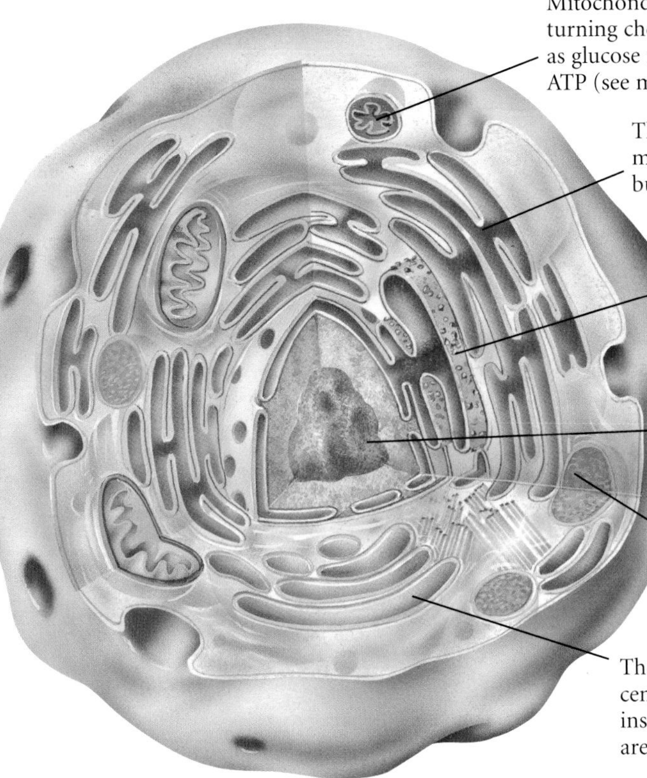

Mitochondria are the cell's power stations, turning chemical fuel supplied by the blood as glucose into energy packs of the chemical ATP (see muscle movement)
The endoplasmic reticulum is the cell's main chemical factory, where proteins are built under instruction from the nucleus
The ribosomes are the individual chemical assembly lines, where proteins are put together from basic chemicals called amino acids (see diet)
The nucleus is the cell's control centre, sending out instructions via a chemical called messenger RNA whenever a new chemical is needed
The lysosomes are the cell's dustbins, breaking up any unwanted material
The Golgi bodies are the cell's despatch centre, where chemicals are bagged up inside tiny membranes to send where they are needed

▲ *This illustration shows a typical cell, and some of the different organelles (special parts of a cell) that keep it working properly. The instructions come from the nucleus in the cell's control centre, but every kind of organelle has its own task.*

FASCINATING FACT

There are 75 trillion cells in your body!

Skin

▲ *Skin colour varies from person to person because of melanin, a pigment which protects skin from the sun's harmful rays. The more melanin you have in your skin, the darker it is.*

- **Skin is your protective coat,** shielding your body from the weather and from infection, and helping to keep it at just the right temperature.
- **Skin is your largest sense receptor**, responding to touch, pressure, heat and cold (see touch).
- **Skin makes** vitamin D for your body from sunlight.
- **The epidermis** (the thin outer layer) is just dead cells.

FASCINATING FACT

Even though its thickness averages just 2 mm, your skin gets an eighth of all your blood supply.

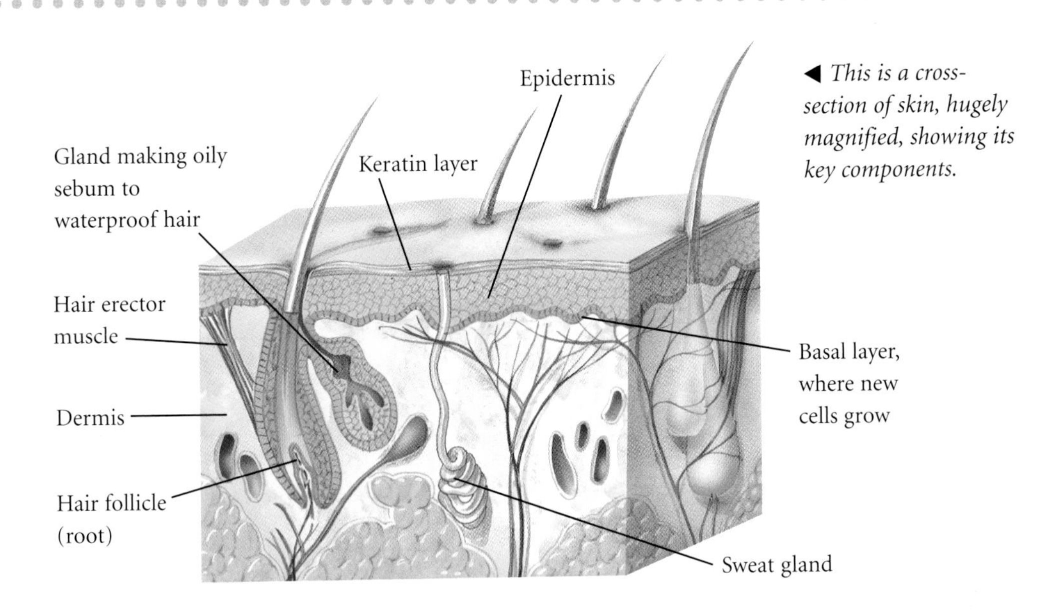

◀ *This is a cross-section of skin, hugely magnified, showing its key components.*

- **The epidermis is made mainly** of a tough protein called keratin – the remains of skin cells that die off.
- **Below the epidermis** is a thick layer of living cells called the dermis, which contains the sweat glands.
- **Hair roots** have tiny muscles that pull the hair upright when you are cold, giving you goose bumps.
- **Skin is 6 mm thick** on the soles of your feet, and just 0.5 mm thick on your eyelids.
- **The epidermis** contains cells that make the dark pigment melanin – this gives dark-skinned people their colour and fair-skinned people a tan.

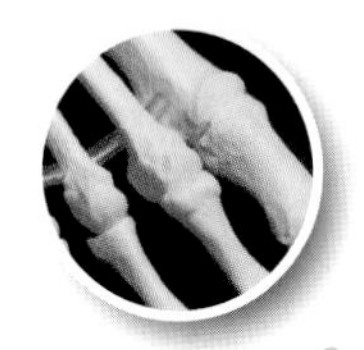

The skeleton

- **Your skeleton** is a rigid framework of bones, which provides an anchor for your muscles, supports your skin and other organs, and protects vital organs.
- **An adult's skeleton has 206 bones** joined together by rubbery cartilage. Some people have extra vertebrae (the bones of the backbone, or spine).
- **A baby's skeleton has 300** or more bones, but some of these fuse (join) together as the baby grows.
- **The parts of an adult skeleton** that have fused into one bone include the skull and the pelvis (see the skull). The pelvis came from fusing the ilium bones, the ischium bones and the pubis. The ischium is the bone that you sit on.

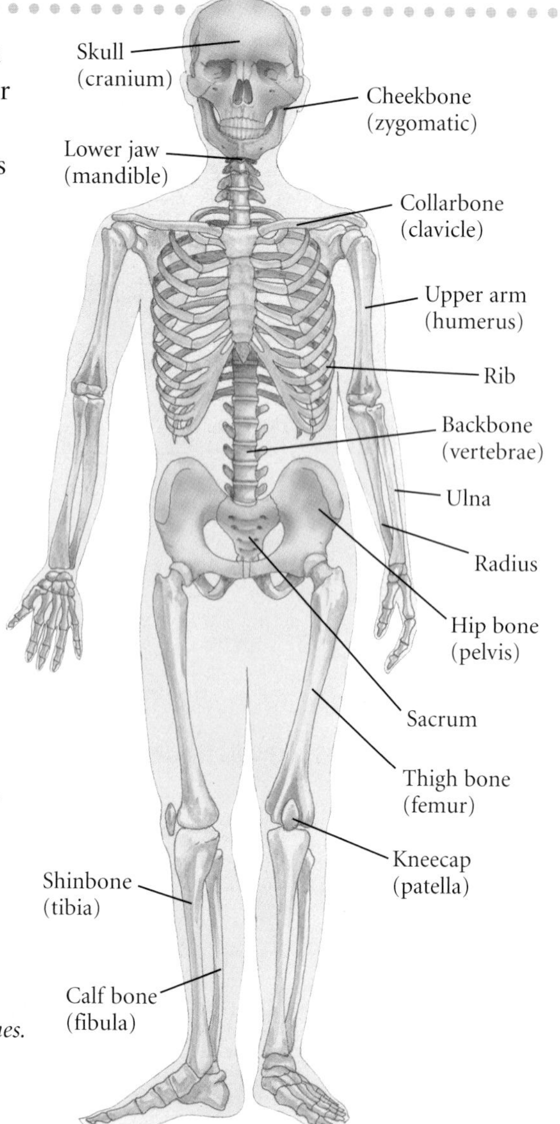

▶ *Your skeleton is the remarkably light, but very tough framework of bones that supports your body. It is made up of more than 200 bones.*

- **The skeleton** has two main parts – the axial and the appendicular skeleton.
- **The axial skeleton** is the 80 bones of the upper body. It includes the skull, the vertebrae of the backbone, the ribs and the breastbone. The arm and shoulder bones are suspended from it.
- **The appendicular skeleton** is the other 126 bones – the arm and shoulder bones, and the leg and hip bones. It includes the femur (thigh bone), the body's longest bone.
- **The word skeleton** comes from the Ancient Greek word for 'dry'.
- **Most women and girls** have smaller and lighter skeletons than men and boys. But in women and girls, the pelvis is much wider than in men and boys. This is because the opening has to be wide enough for a baby to pass through when it is born.

▲ *There are 19 bones in the toes and foot, and 6 in the ankle, making 25 bones altogether that can be seen in this photograph.*

FASCINATING FACT

The tiniest bone in your body is only 3 mm long and is found in your ear.

Bone

- **Bones are so strong** that they can cope with twice the squeezing pressure that granite can, or four times the stretching tension that concrete can.
- **Weight for weight,** bone is at least five times as strong as steel.
- **Bones are so light** they only make up 14% of your body's total weight.
- **Bones get their rigidity** from hard deposits of minerals such as calcium and phosphate.

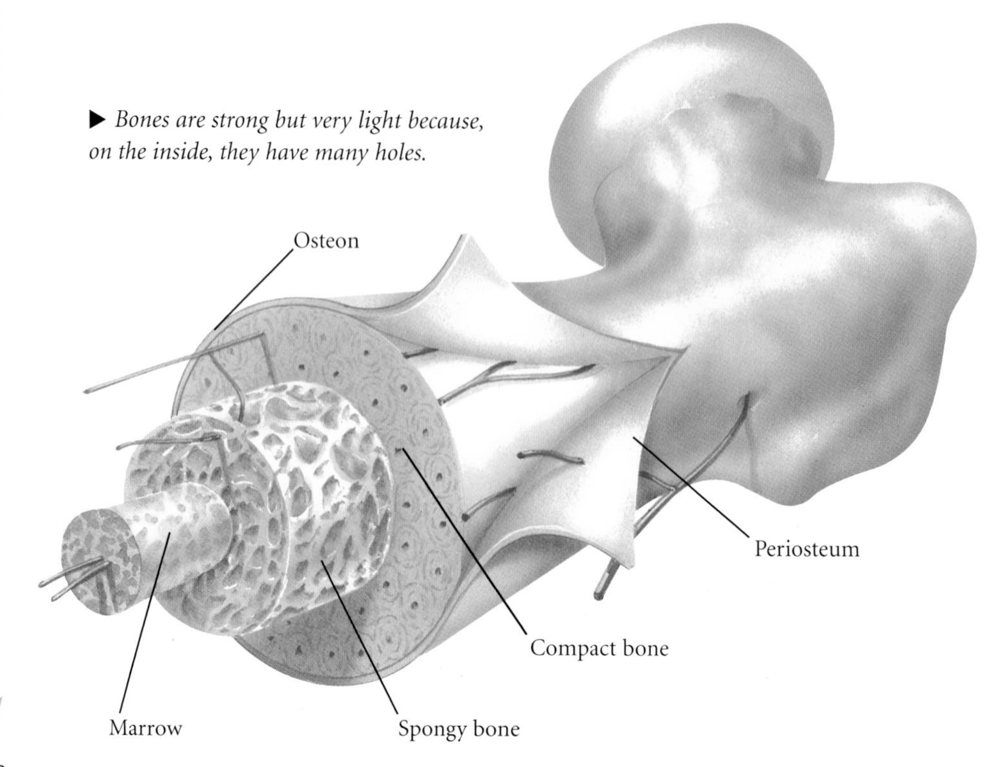

▶ *Bones are strong but very light because, on the inside, they have many holes.*

- **Bones get their flexibility** from tough, elastic, rope-like fibres of collagen.
- **The hard outside of bones** (called compact bone) is reinforced by strong rods called osteons.
- **The inside of bones** (called spongy bone) is a light honeycomb, made of thin struts or trabeculae, perfectly angled to take stress.
- **The core of some bones,** such as the long bones in an arm or leg, is called bone marrow. It is soft and jelly-like.
- **In some parts of each bone,** there are special cells called osteoblasts which make new bone. In other parts, cells called osteoclasts break up old bone.
- **Bones grow** by getting longer near the end, at a region called the epiphyseal plate.

▲ *Milk contains a mineral called calcium, which is essential for building strong bones. Babies and children need plenty of calcium to help their bones develop properly.*

Muscles

- **Muscles are special fibres** that contract (tighten) and relax to move parts of the body.

FASCINATING FACT

The body's smallest muscle is the stapedius, inside the ear.

- **Voluntary muscles** are all the muscles you can control by will or thinking, such as your arm muscles.
- **Involuntary muscles** are the muscles you cannot control at will, but work automatically, such as the muscles that move food through your intestine.
- **Most voluntary muscles** cover the skeleton and are therefore called skeletal muscles. They are also called striated (striped) muscle because there are dark bands on the bundles of fibre that form them.
- **Most involuntary muscles** form sacs or tubes such as the intestine or the blood vessels. They are called smooth muscle because they lack the bands or stripes of voluntary muscles.

▶ *This microscopic cross-section shows striated, or striped, skeletal muscle. It is so-called because its fibres are made of light and dark stripes.*

- **Most muscles are arranged in pairs,** because although muscles can shorten themselves, they cannot forcibly make themselves longer. So the flexor muscle that bends a joint is paired with an extensor muscle to straighten it out again.
- **Heart muscle** is a unique combination of skeletal and smooth muscle. It has its own built-in contraction rhythm of 70 beats a minute, and special muscle cells that work like nerve cells for transmitting the signals for waves of muscle contraction to sweep through the heart.
- **Your body's longest muscle** is the sartorius on the inner thigh.
- **Your body's widest muscle** is the external oblique which runs around the side of the upper body.
- **Your body's biggest muscle** is the gluteus maximus in your buttock (bottom).

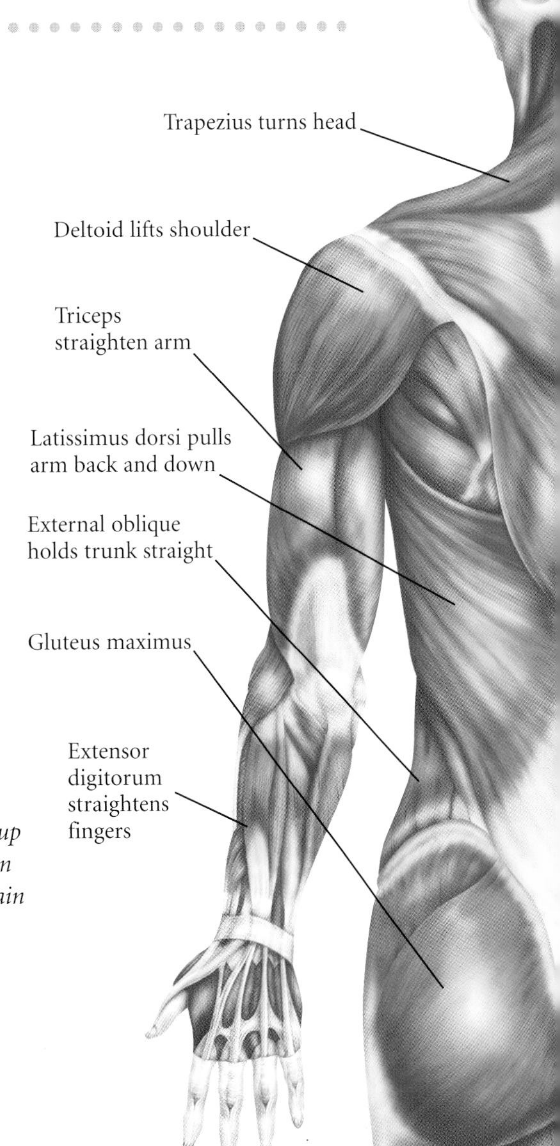

▶ *You have more than 640 skeletal muscles and they make up over 40% of your body's entire weight, covering your skeleton like a bulky blanket. The illustration here shows only the main surface muscles of the back, but your body has at least two layers, and sometimes three layers, of muscle beneath its surface muscles. Most muscles are firmly anchored at both ends and attached to the bones either side of a joint, either directly or via tough fibres called tendons.*

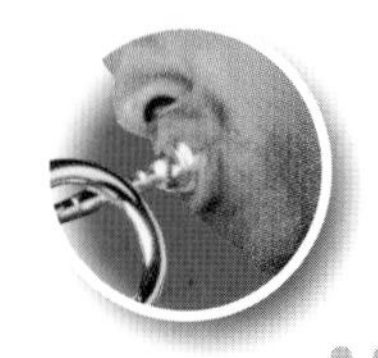

Breathing

- **You breathe** because every single cell in your body needs a continuous supply of oxygen to burn glucose, the high-energy substance from digested food that cells get from blood.
- **Scientists** call breathing 'respiration'. Cellular respiration is the way that cells use oxygen to burn glucose.
- **The oxygen in air** is taken into your lungs, and then carried in your blood to your body cells.
- **Waste carbon dioxide** from your cells is returned by your blood to your lungs, to be breathed out.
- **On average** you breathe in about 15 times a minute. If you run hard, the rate soars to around 80 times a minute.

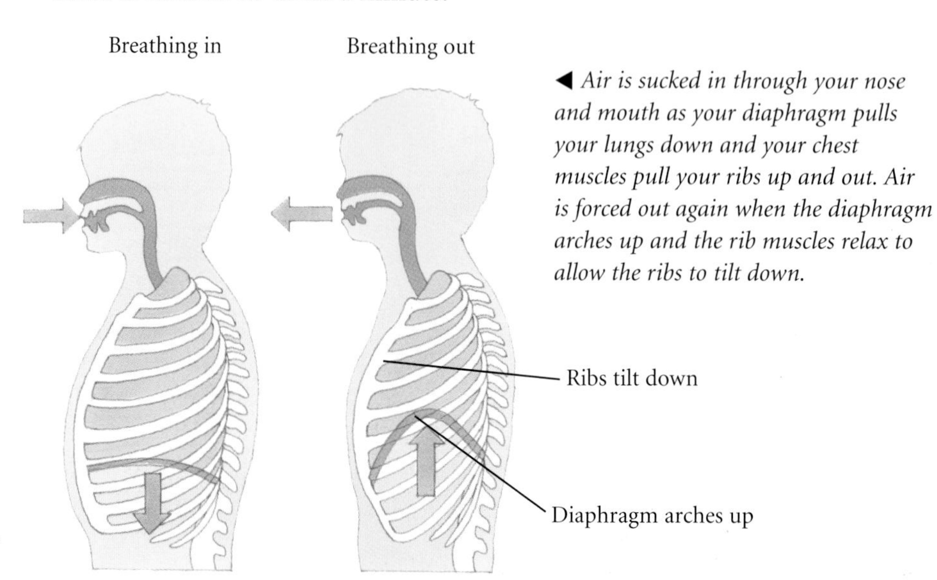

◀ *Air is sucked in through your nose and mouth as your diaphragm pulls your lungs down and your chest muscles pull your ribs up and out. Air is forced out again when the diaphragm arches up and the rib muscles relax to allow the ribs to tilt down.*

- **Newborn babies** breathe about 40 times a minute.
- **If you live to the age of 80,** you will have taken well over 600 million breaths.
- **A normal breath** takes in about 0.4 litres of air. A deep breath can take in ten times as much.
- **Your diaphragm** is a dome-shaped sheet of muscle between your chest and stomach, which works with your chest muscles to make you breathe in and out.

- **Scientists** call breathing in 'inhalation', and breathing out 'exhalation'.

▶ *Wind musicians, such as this trumpeter, use their diaphragm and chest to control the air flowing in and out of their lungs. This allows them to produce a better quality sound.*

The lungs

FASCINATING FACT
Opened out and laid flat, the alveoli would cover half a football field.

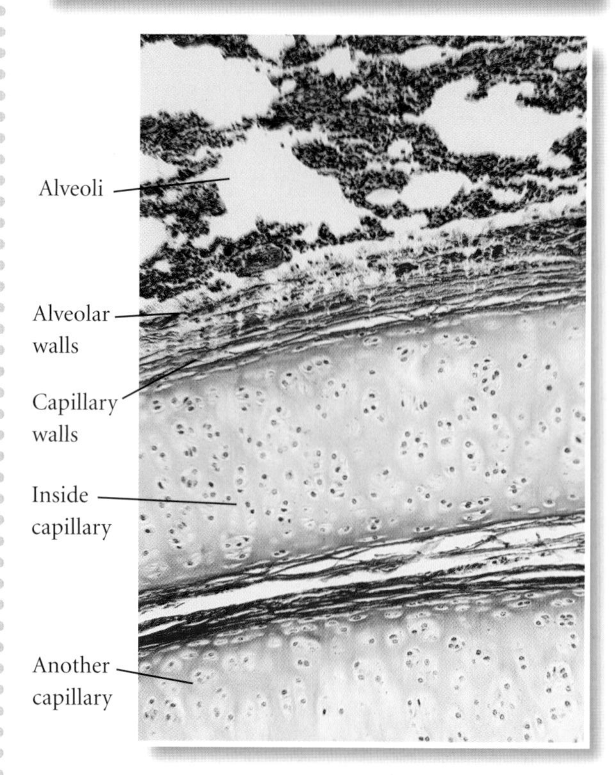

▲ *Taken through a powerful microscope, this photo of a slice of lung tissue shows a blood vessel and the very thin walls of an alveolus next to it.*

- **Your lungs** are a pair of soft, spongy bags inside your chest.
- **When you breathe** in, air rushes in through your nose or mouth, down your windpipe and into the millions of branching airways in your lungs.
- **The two biggest airways** are called bronchi (singular bronchus), and they both branch into smaller airways called bronchioles.
- **The surface of your airways** is protected by a slimy film of mucus, which gets thicker to protect the lungs when you have a cold.

- **At the end of each bronchiole** are bunches of minute air sacs called alveoli (singular alveolus).
- **Alveoli** are wrapped around with tiny blood vessels, and alveoli walls are just one cell thick – thin enough to let oxygen and carbon dioxide seep through them.
- **There are around 300 million alveoli** in your lungs.
- **The large surface area** of all these alveoli makes it possible for huge quantities of oxygen to seep through into the blood. Equally huge quantities of carbon dioxide can seep back into the airways for removal when you breathe out.

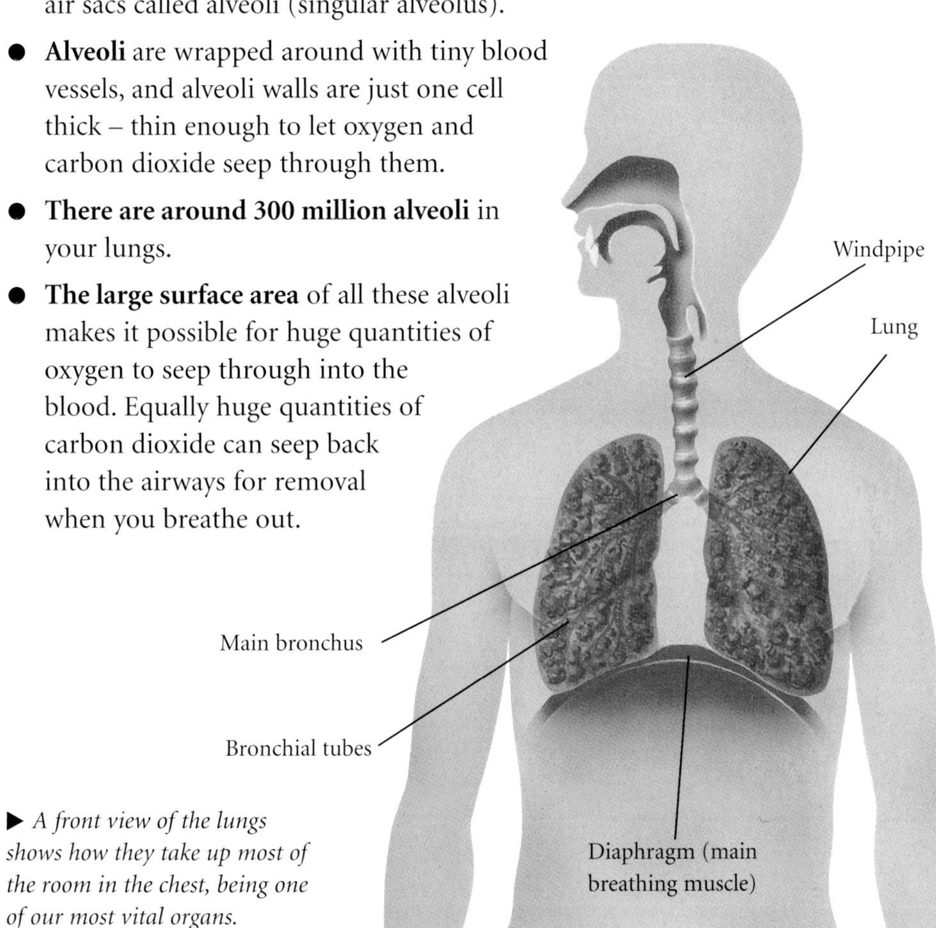

▶ *A front view of the lungs shows how they take up most of the room in the chest, being one of our most vital organs.*

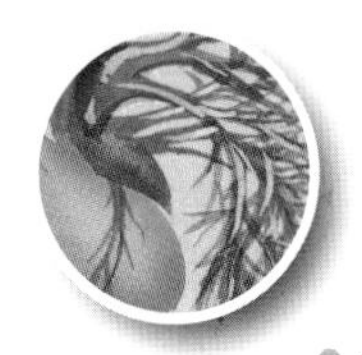

Circulation

> **. . . FASCINATING FACT . . .**
> It takes less than 90 seconds on average for the blood to circulate through all of the body's 100,000 km of blood vessels!

- **Your circulation** is the system of tubes called blood vessels which carries blood out from your heart to all your body cells and back again.
- **Blood circulation** was discovered in 1628 by the English physician William Harvey (1578–1657), who built on the ideas of Matteo Colombo.
- **Each of the body's** 600 billion cells gets fresh blood continuously, although the blood flow is pulsating.
- **On the way out** from the heart, blood is pumped through vessels called arteries and arterioles.
- **On the way back** to the heart, blood flows through venules and veins.
- **Blood flows** from the arterioles to the venules through the tiniest tubes called capillaries.
- **The blood circulation** has two parts – the pulmonary and the systemic.
- **The pulmonary circulation** is the short section that carries blood which is low in oxygen from the right side of the heart to the lungs for 'refuelling'. It then returns oxygen-rich blood to the left side of the heart.
- **The systemic circulation** carries oxygen-rich blood from the left side of the heart all around the body, and returns blood which is low in oxygen to the right side of the heart.
- **Inside the blood,** oxygen is carried by the haemoglobin in red blood cells (see blood cells).

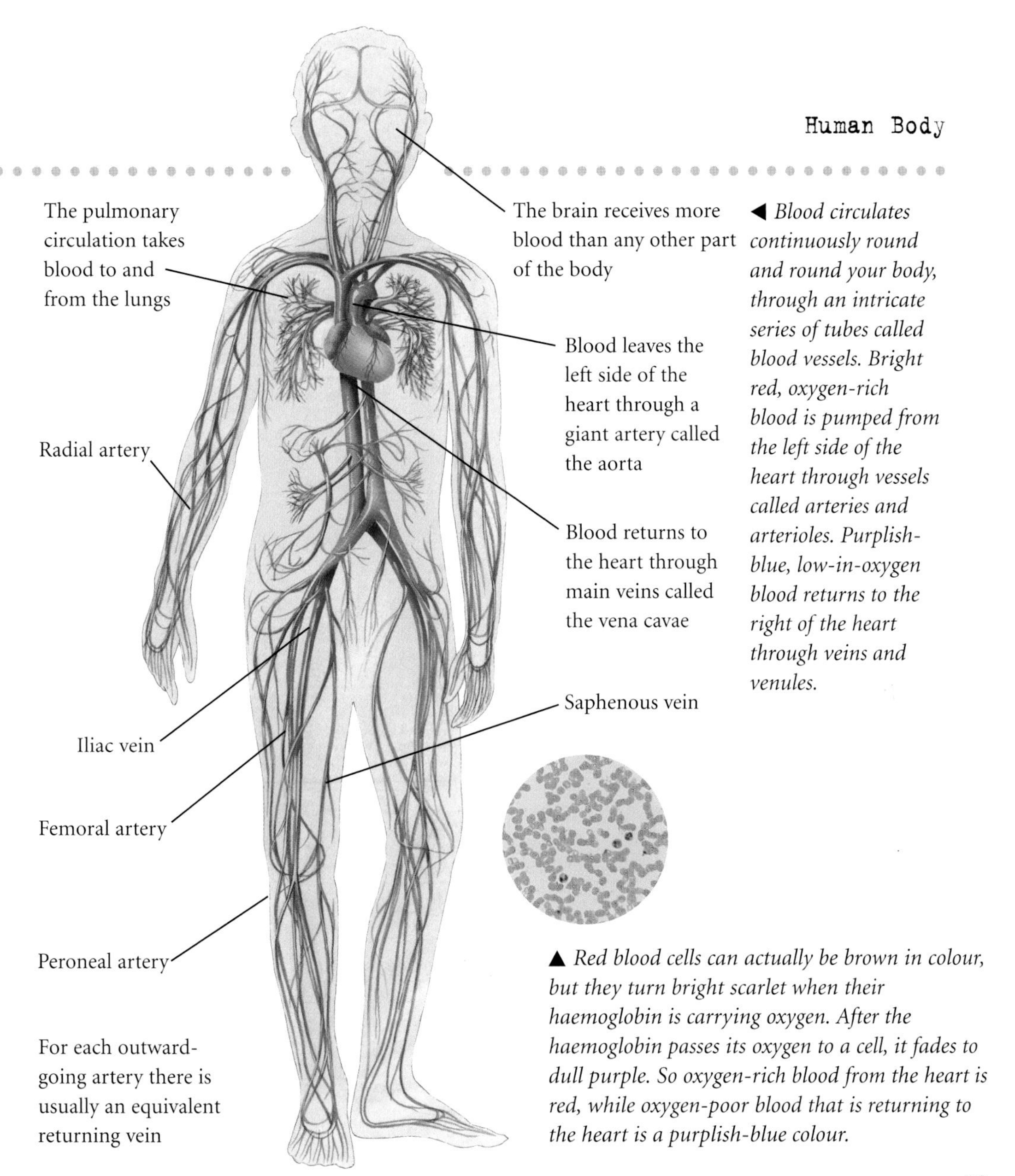
The pulmonary circulation takes blood to and from the lungs
Radial artery
Iliac vein
Femoral artery
Peroneal artery
For each outward-going artery there is usually an equivalent returning vein
The brain receives more blood than any other part of the body
Blood leaves the left side of the heart through a giant artery called the aorta
Blood returns to the heart through main veins called the vena cavae
Saphenous vein

◀ *Blood circulates continuously round and round your body, through an intricate series of tubes called blood vessels. Bright red, oxygen-rich blood is pumped from the left side of the heart through vessels called arteries and arterioles. Purplish-blue, low-in-oxygen blood returns to the right of the heart through veins and venules.*

▲ *Red blood cells can actually be brown in colour, but they turn bright scarlet when their haemoglobin is carrying oxygen. After the haemoglobin passes its oxygen to a cell, it fades to dull purple. So oxygen-rich blood from the heart is red, while oxygen-poor blood that is returning to the heart is a purplish-blue colour.*

The heart

- **Your heart** is the size of your fist. It is inside the middle of your chest, slightly to the left.
- **The heart is a powerful pump** made almost entirely of muscle.
- **The heart contracts** (tightens) and relaxes automatically about 70 times a minute to pump blood out through your arteries.
- **The heart has two sides** separated by a muscle wall called the septum.
- **The right side** is smaller and weaker, and it pumps blood only to the lungs.
- **The stronger left side** pumps blood around the body.
- **Each side of the heart** has two chambers. There is an atrium (plural atria) at the top where blood accumulates (builds up) from the veins, and a ventricle below which contracts to pump blood out into the arteries.
- **Each side of the heart** (left and right) ejects about 70 ml of blood every beat.
- **There are two valves** in each side of the heart to make sure that blood flows only one way – a large one between the atrium and the ventricle, and a small one at the exit from the ventricle into the artery.
- **The coronary arteries** supply the heart. If they become clogged, the heart muscle may be short of blood and stop working. This is what happens in a heart attack.

... FASCINATING FACT ...

During an average lifetime, the heart pumps 200 million litres of blood – enough to fill New York's Central Park to a depth of 15 m.

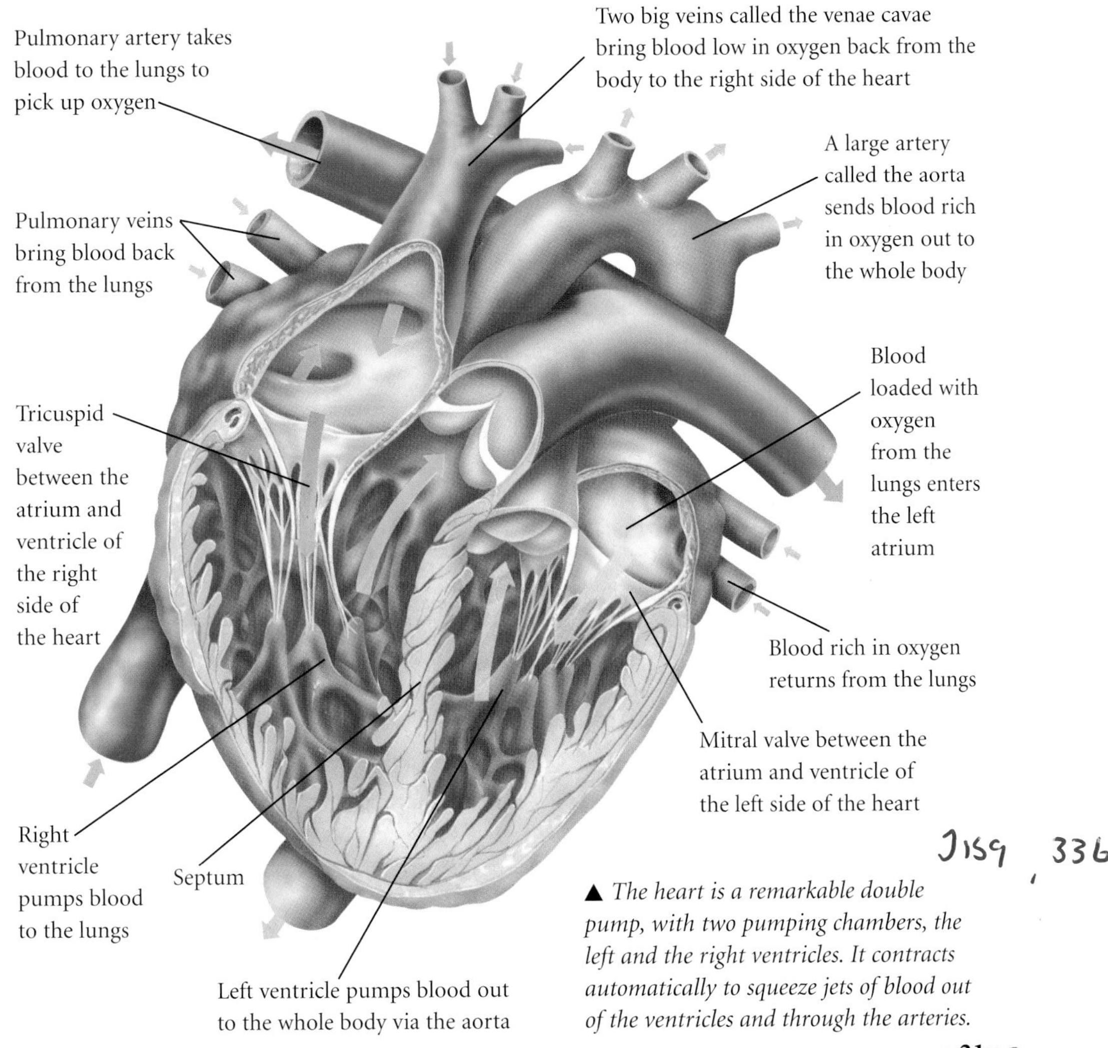
Pulmonary artery takes blood to the lungs to pick up oxygen
Two big veins called the venae cavae bring blood low in oxygen back from the body to the right side of the heart
A large artery called the aorta sends blood rich in oxygen out to the whole body
Pulmonary veins bring blood back from the lungs
Blood loaded with oxygen from the lungs enters the left atrium
Tricuspid valve between the atrium and ventricle of the right side of the heart
Blood rich in oxygen returns from the lungs
Mitral valve between the atrium and ventricle of the left side of the heart
Right ventricle pumps blood to the lungs
Septum
Left ventricle pumps blood out to the whole body via the aorta

▲ *The heart is a remarkable double pump, with two pumping chambers, the left and the right ventricles. It contracts automatically to squeeze jets of blood out of the ventricles and through the arteries.*

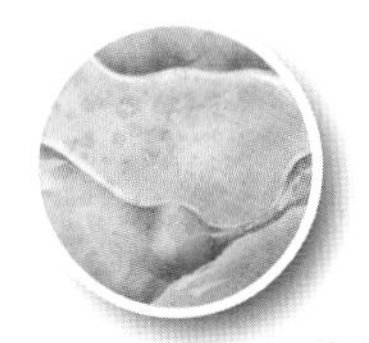

Blood cells

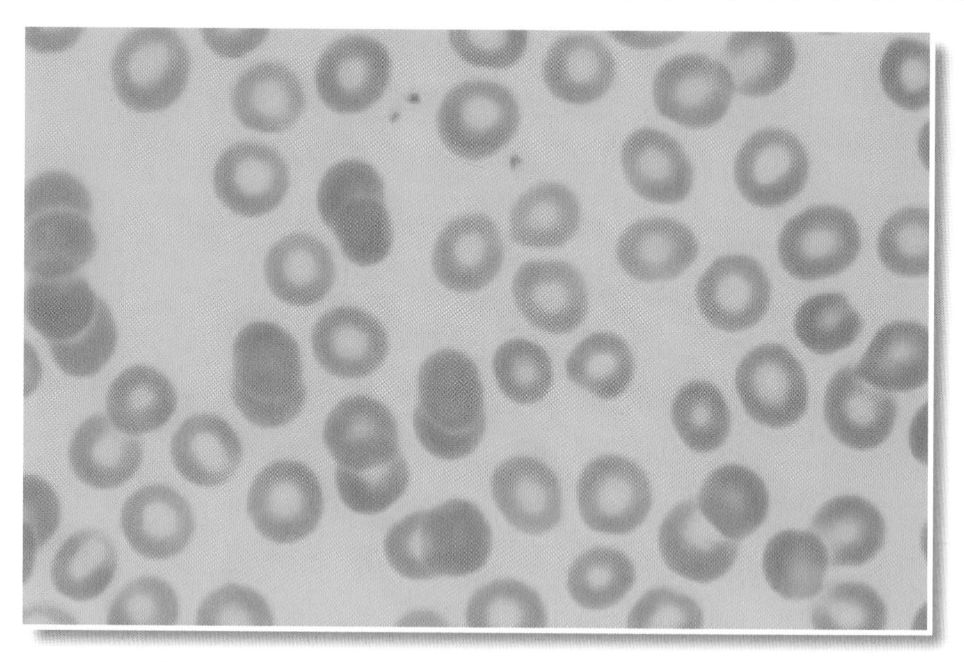

▲ *This is a highly magnified photograph of red blood cells.*

- **Your blood has two main kinds of cell** – red cells and white cells – plus pieces of cell called platelets (see blood).
- **Red cells** are button-shaped and they contain mainly a red protein called haemoglobin.
- **Haemoglobin** is what allows red blood cells to ferry oxygen around your body.
- **Red cells** also contain enzymes which the body uses to make certain chemical processes happen (see enzymes).

- **White blood cells** are big cells called leucocytes and most types are involved in fighting infections.
- **Most white cells** contain tiny little grains and are called granulocytes.
- **Most granulocytes** are giant white cells called neutrophils. They are the blood's cleaners, and their task is to eat up invaders.
- **Eosinophils and basophils** are granulocytes that are involved in fighting disease. Some release antibodies that help fight infection (see antibodies).
- **Lymphocytes** are also types of white cells (see lymphocytes and antibodies).

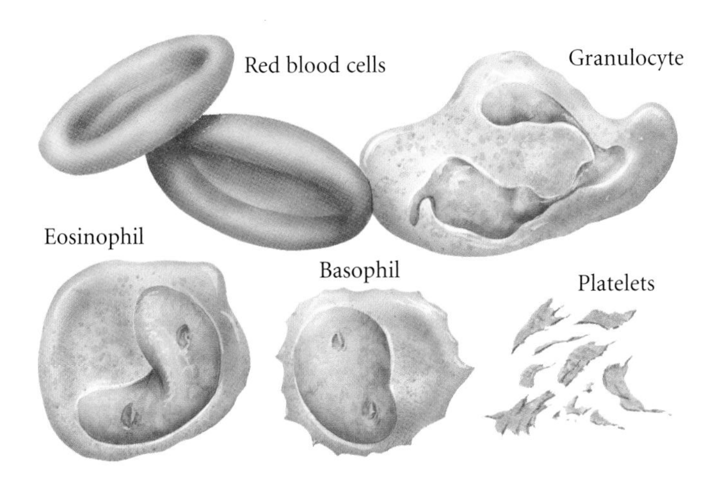

▲ *These are some important kinds of cell in the blood – red cells, three kinds of white cells, and platelets.*

... FASCINATING FACT ...
Each red blood cell contains more than 200 million molecules of haemoglobin.

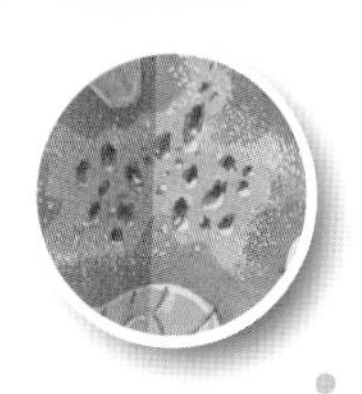

The lymphatic system

- **The lymphatic system** is your body's sewer, the network of pipes that drains waste from the cells.
- **The 'pipes' of the lymphatic system** are called lymphatics or lymph vessels.
- **The lymphatics** are filled by a watery liquid called lymph fluid which, along with bacteria and waste chemicals, drains from body tissues such as muscles.
- **The lymphatic system** has no pump, such as the heart, to make it circulate. Instead, lymphatic fluid is circulated as a side effect of the heartbeat and muscle movement.

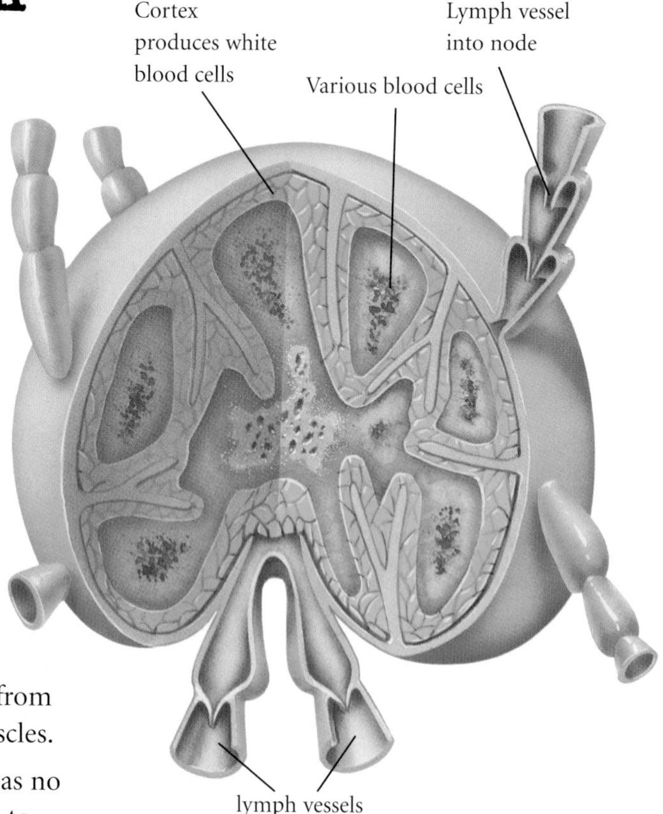

▲ *This shows a cross-section of a lymph node. White blood cells are produced and stored here, and are released through the lymph vessels into the bloodstream.*

- **At places** in the lymphatic system there are tiny lumps called nodes. These are filters which trap germs that have got into the lymph fluid.
- **In the nodes**, armies of white blood cells called lymphocytes neutralize or destroy germs.
- **When you have** a cold or any other infection, the lymph nodes in your neck or groin, or under your arm, may swell, as lymphocytes fight germs. This is sometimes called 'swollen glands'.
- **Lymph fluid** drains back into the blood via the body's main vein, the superior vena cava (see heart).
- **The lymphatic system** is not only the lymphatics and lymph nodes, but includes the spleen, the thymus, the tonsils and the adenoids (see the immune system).
- **On average**, at any time about 1 to 2 litres of lymph fluid circulate in the lymphatics and body tissues.

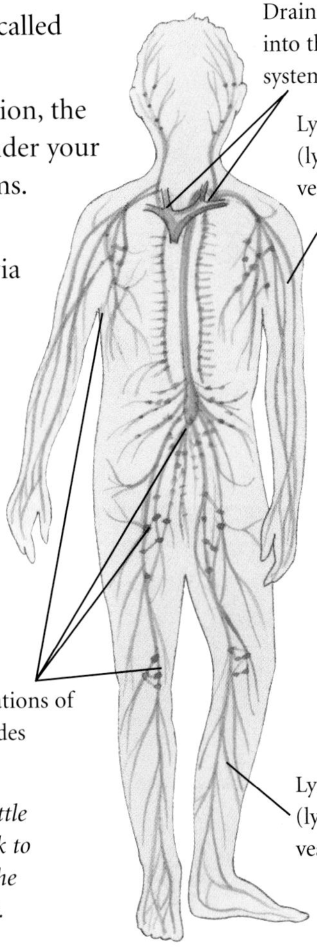

▶ *The lymphatic system is a branching network of little tubes that reaches throughout the body. It drains back to the centre of the body, running into the branches of the superior vena cava, the body's main vein to the heart.*

Digestion

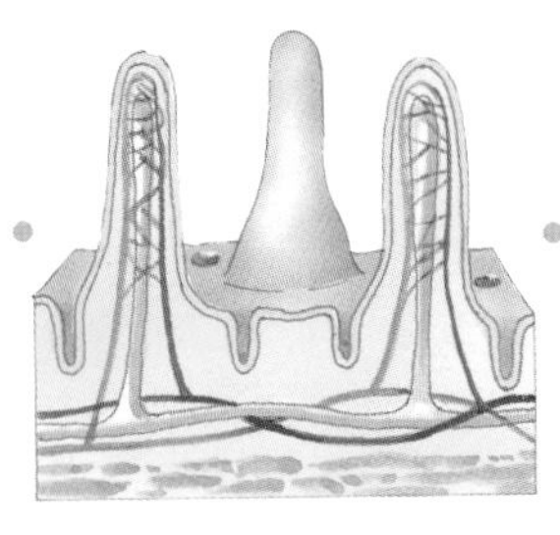

▲ *The small intestine is lined with tiny, finger-like folds called villi. On the surface of each villus are even tinier, finger-like folds called microvilli. These folds give a huge area for absorbing food.*

- **Digestion** is the process by which your body breaks down the food you eat into substances that it can absorb (take in) and use.
- **Your digestive tract** is basically a long, winding tube called the alimentary canal (gut). It starts at your mouth and ends at your anus.
- **If you could lay** your gut out straight, it would be nearly six times as long as you are tall.
- **The food you eat** is softened in your mouth by chewing and by chemicals in your saliva (spit).
- **When you swallow,** food travels down your oesophagus (gullet) into your stomach. Your stomach is a muscular-walled bag which mashes the food into a pulp, helped by chemicals called gastric juices.
- **When empty,** your stomach holds barely 0.5 litres, but after a big meal it can stretch to more than 4 litres.
- **The half-digested food** that leaves your stomach is called chyme. It passes into your small intestine.
- **Your small intestine** is a 6-m-long tube where chyme is broken down into molecules small enough to be absorbed through the intestine wall into the blood.

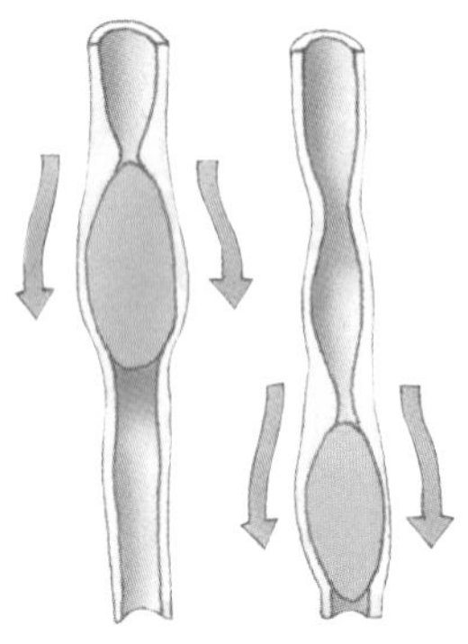

▲ *Food is pushed through the long, winding digestive tract by waves of contraction (tightening) that pass along its muscular walls. These waves are called peristalsis.*

... FASCINATING FACT ...

On average, food takes 24 hours to pass right the way through your alimentary canal and out the other end.

- **Food that cannot be** digested in your small intestine passes on into your large intestine. It is then pushed out through your anus as faeces when you go to the toilet (see excretion).
- **Digestive enzymes** play a vital part in breaking food down so it can be absorbed by the body.

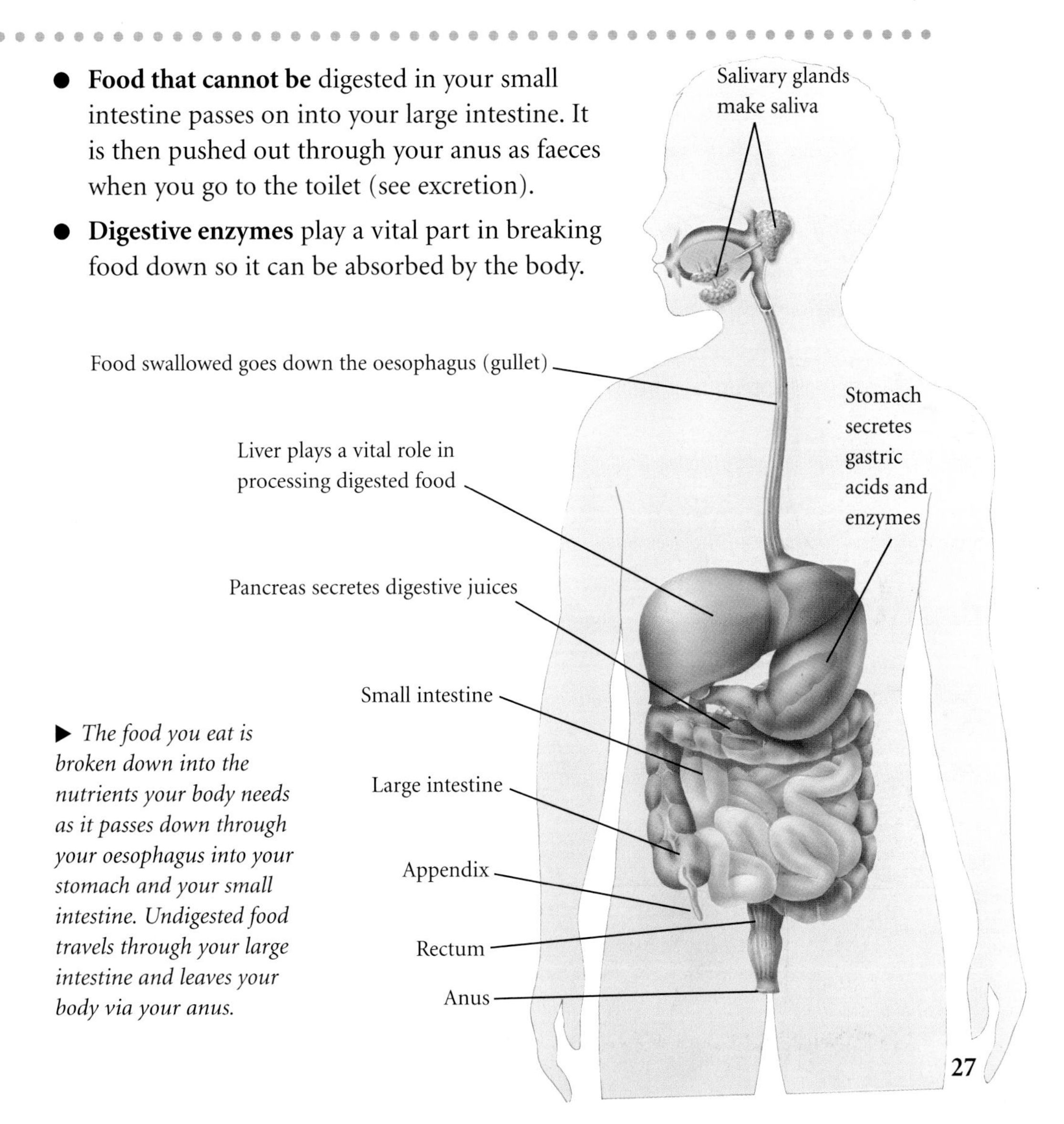

▶ *The food you eat is broken down into the nutrients your body needs as it passes down through your oesophagus into your stomach and your small intestine. Undigested food travels through your large intestine and leaves your body via your anus.*

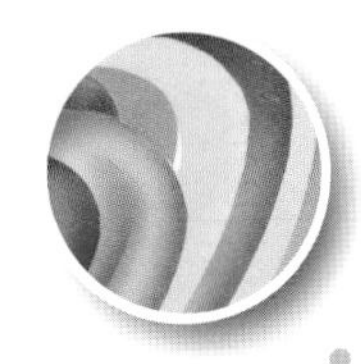

The brain

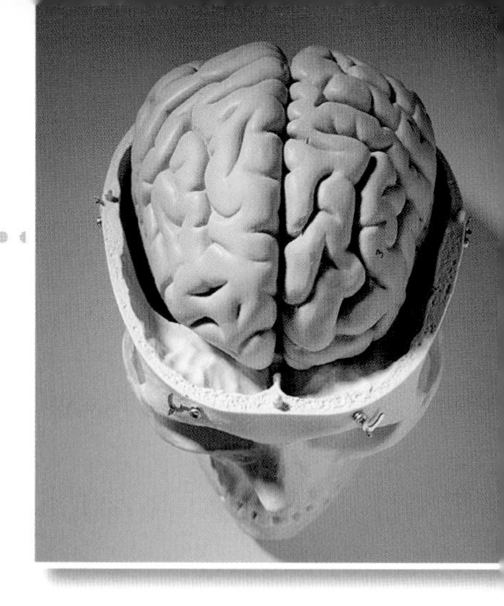

▲ *Taking the top off the skull shows the brain to be a soggy, pinky-grey mass which looks rather like a giant walnut*

- **The human brain** is made up of more than 100 billion nerve cells called neurons.
- **Each neuron** is connected to as many as 25,000 other neurons – so the brain has trillions and trillions of different pathways for nerve signals.
- **Girls' brains** weigh 2.5% of their body weight, on average, while boys' brains weigh 2%.
- **About 0.85 litres** of blood shoots through your brain every minute. The brain may be as little as 2% of your body weight, but it demands 12–15% of your blood supply.
- **An elephant's brain** weighs four times as much as the human brain. Some apes, monkeys and dolphins are quite near our brain–body ratio.
- **The cerebral cortex** is the outside of the brain, and if it was laid out flat, it would cover a bed.
- **The left hemisphere (half)** of the upper part of the brain is more dominant in speech, writing and general language, the right half in pictures and ideas.
- **Conscious thoughts and actions** happen in the cerebral cortex.
- **A human brain** has a cerebral cortex four times as big as a chimpanzee, about 20 times as big as a monkey's, and about 300 times as big as a rat's.
- **Unconscious, automatic activities** such as breathing, hunger, sleep and so on are controlled by structures such as the hypothalamus and the brain stem.

...FASCINATING FACT...

Scientists can now grow human brain cells in a laboratory dish.

▶ *In this illustration, the right hemisphere (half) of the cerebrum is shown in pink, surrounding the regions that control basic drives such as hunger, thirst and anger.*

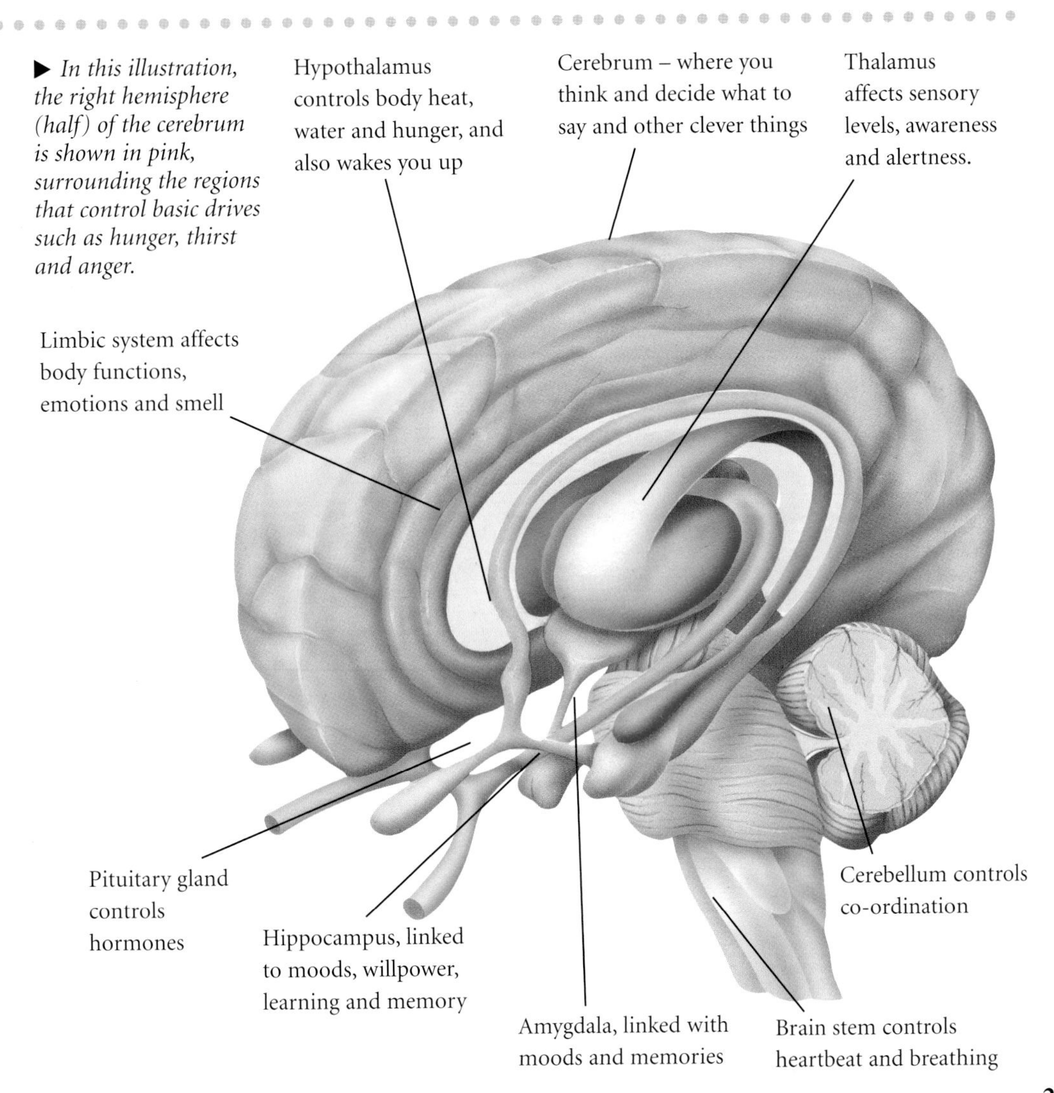
Hypothalamus controls body heat, water and hunger, and also wakes you up
Cerebrum – where you think and decide what to say and other clever things
Thalamus affects sensory levels, awareness and alertness.
Limbic system affects body functions, emotions and smell
Pituitary gland controls hormones
Hippocampus, linked to moods, willpower, learning and memory
Amygdala, linked with moods and memories
Brain stem controls heartbeat and breathing
Cerebellum controls co-ordination

The eye

- **Your eyes** are tough balls that are filled with a jelly-like substance called vitreous humour.
- **The cornea** is a thin, glassy dish across the front of your eye. It allows light rays through the eye's window, the pupil, and into the lens.
- **The iris** is the coloured, muscular ring around the pupil. The iris narrows in bright light and widens when light is dim.
- **The lens** is just behind the pupil. It focuses the picture of the world on to the back of the eye.
- **The back of the eye** is lined with millions of light-sensitive cells. This lining is called the retina, and it registers the picture and sends signals to the brain via the optic nerve.
- **There are two kinds** of light-sensitive cell in the retina – rods and cones. Rods are very sensitive and work in even dim light, but they cannot detect colours. Cones respond to colour.
- **Some kinds of cone** are very sensitive to red light, some to green and some to blue. One theory says that the colours we see depend on how strongly they affect each of these three kinds of cone (see colour vision).
- **Each of your two eyes** gives you a slightly different view of the world. The brain combines these views to give an impression of depth and 3-D solidity.
- **Although each eye** gives a slightly different view of the world, we see things largely as just one eye sees it. This dominant eye is usually the right eye.

...FASCINATING FACT...

The picture received by your retina looks large and real – yet it is upside down and just a few millimetres across.

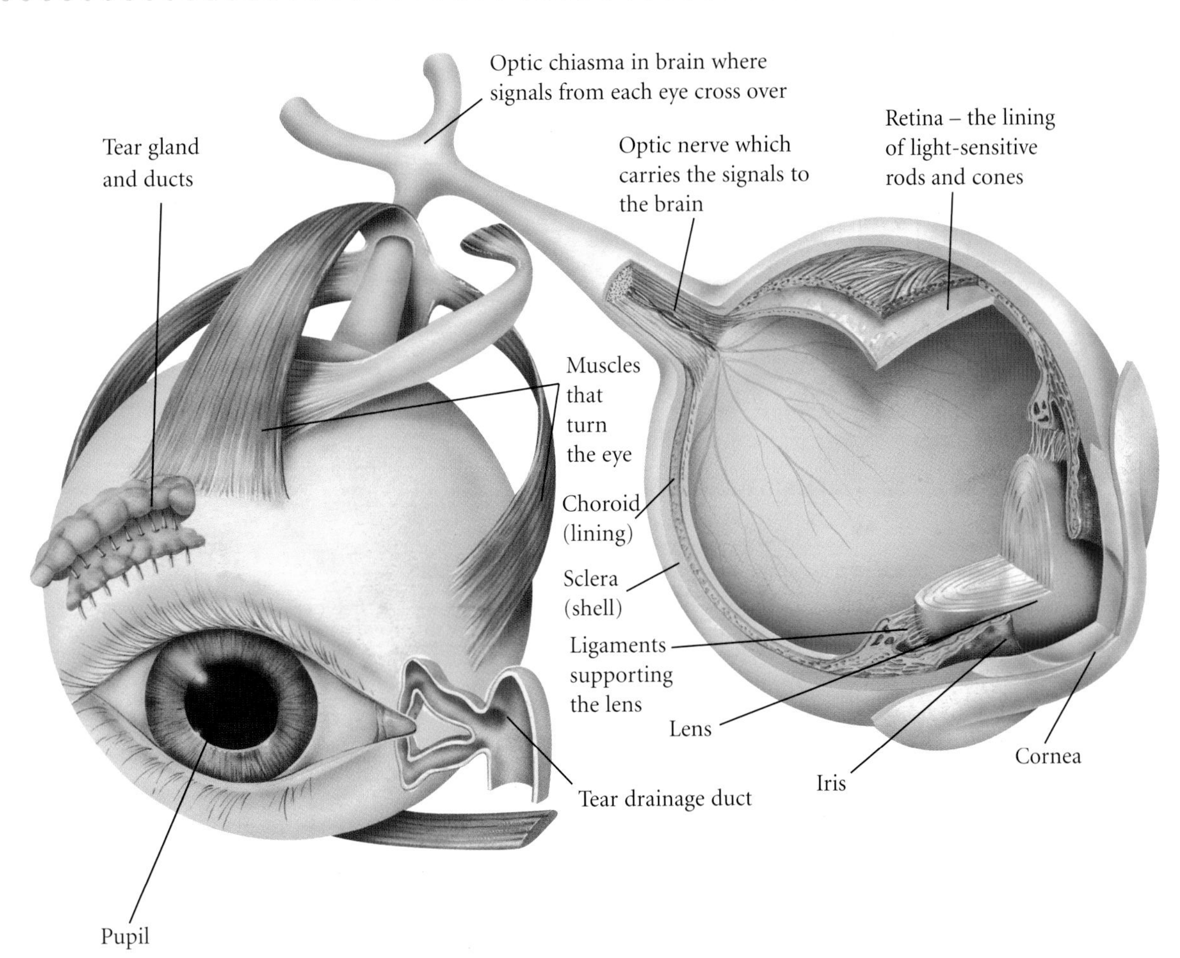

▲ *This illustration shows your two eyeballs, with a cutaway to reveal the cornea and lens (which projects light rays through the eye's window) and the light-sensitive retina (which registers it).*

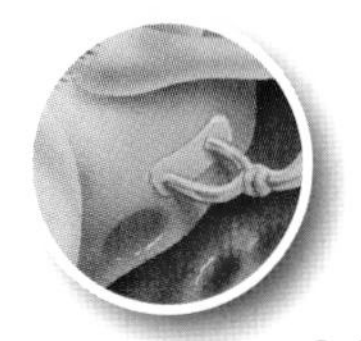

The ear

- **Pinnae** (singular, pinna) are the ear flaps you can see on the side of your head, and they are simply collecting funnels for sounds.

...FASCINATING FACT...

If your hearing is normal, you can hear sounds as deep as 20 Hertz (Hz) – vibrations per second – and as high as 20,000 Hz.

- **A little way inside your head,** sounds hit a thin, tight wall of skin, called the eardrum, making it vibrate.
- **When the eardrum vibrates,** it shakes three little bones called ossicles. These are the smallest bones in the body.
- **The three ossicle bones** are the malleus (hammer), the incus (anvil) and the stapes (stirrup).
- **When the ossicles vibrate,** they rattle a tiny membrane called the oval window, intensifying the vibration.
- **The oval window** is 30 times smaller in area than the eardrum.
- **Beyond the oval window** is the cochlea – a winding collection of three, liquid-filled tubes, which looks a bit like a snail shell.
- **In the middle tube** of the cochlea there is a flap which covers row upon row of tiny hairs. This is called the organ of Corti.
- **When sounds make** the eardrum vibrate, the ossicles tap on the oval window, making pressure waves shoot through the liquid in the cochlea and wash over the flap of the organ of Corti, waving it up and down.
- **When the organ of Corti waves,** it tugs on the tiny hairs under the flap. These send signals to the brain via the auditory nerve, and you hear a sound.

▼ *Most of your ear is hidden inside your head. It is an amazingly complex and delicate structure for picking up the tiny variations in air pressure created by a sound.*

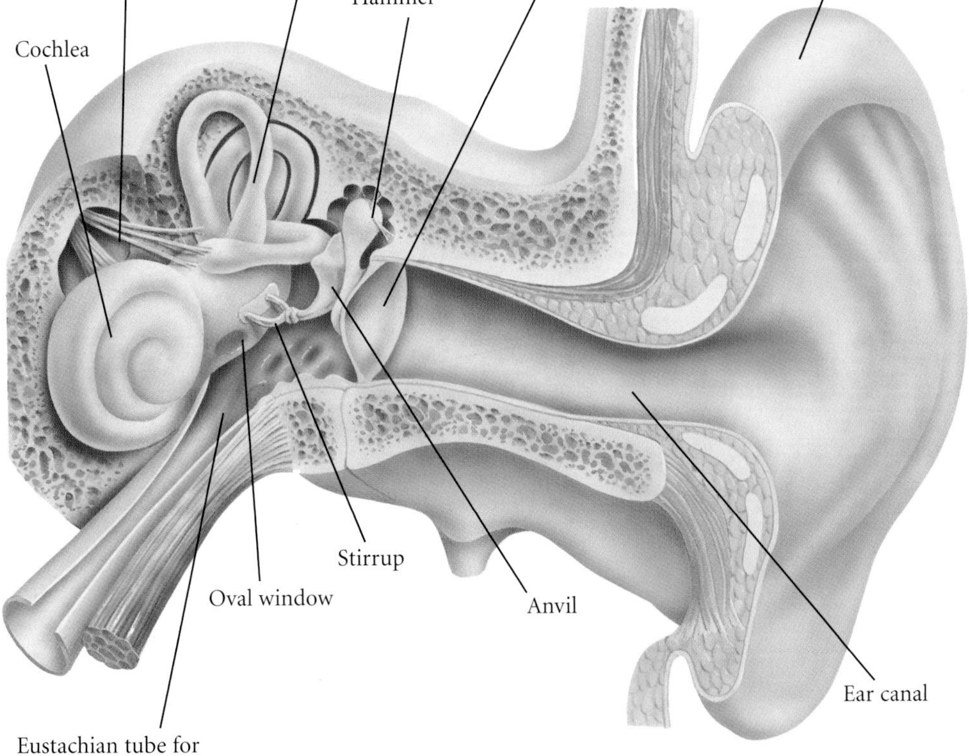

Auditory nerve

Liquid-filled semi-circular canals help you to balance

Eardrum

Ear flap

Hammer

Cochlea

Stirrup

Oval window

Anvil

Ear canal

Eustachian tube for relieving air pressure

Smell

- **Smells are scent molecules** which are taken into your nose by breathed-in air. A particular smell may be noticeable even when just a single scent molecule is mixed in with millions of air molecules.
- **The human nose** can tell the difference between more than 10,000 different chemicals.
- **Dogs can pick up** smells that are 10,000 times fainter than the ones humans can detect.
- **Inside the nose,** scent molecules are picked up by a patch of scent-sensitive cells called the olfactory epithelium.
- **Olfactory** means 'to do with the sense of smell'.
- **The olfactory epithelium** contains over 25 million receptor cells.

▲ *Scents are closely linked to emotions in the brain, and perfume can be a powerful way of triggering feelings.*

- **Each of the receptor cells** in the olfactory epithelium has up to 20 or so scent-detecting hairs called cilia.
- **When they are triggered** by scent molecules, the cilia send signals to a cluster of nerves called the olfactory bulb, which then sends messages to the part of the brain that recognizes smell.
- **The part of the brain** that deals with smell is closely linked to the parts that deal with memories and emotions. This may be why smells can often evoke vivid memories.
- **By the age of 20,** you will have lost 20% of your sense of smell. By 60, you will have lost 60% of it.

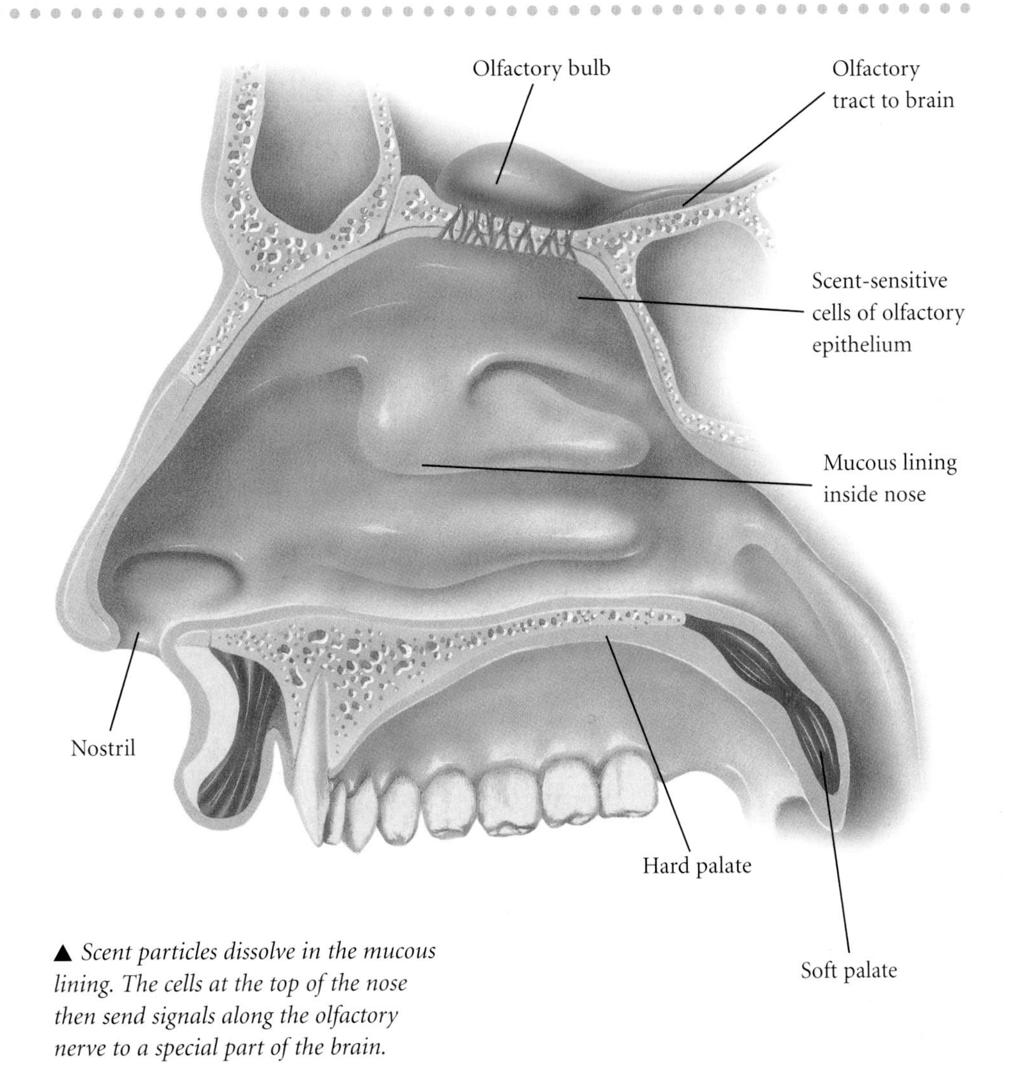

▲ *Scent particles dissolve in the mucous lining. The cells at the top of the nose then send signals along the olfactory nerve to a special part of the brain.*

Taste

▲ *As well as tasting the flavour of ice cream, the tongue can also tell that it is cold and smooth.*

- **The sense of taste** is the crudest of our five senses, giving us less information about the world than any other sense.
- **Taste** is triggered by certain chemicals in food, which dissolve in the saliva in your mouth, and then send information to a particular part of the brain via sensory nerve cells on the tongue.

▶ *Certain parts of the tongue are more sensitive to one flavour than to others, as shown in this diagram.*

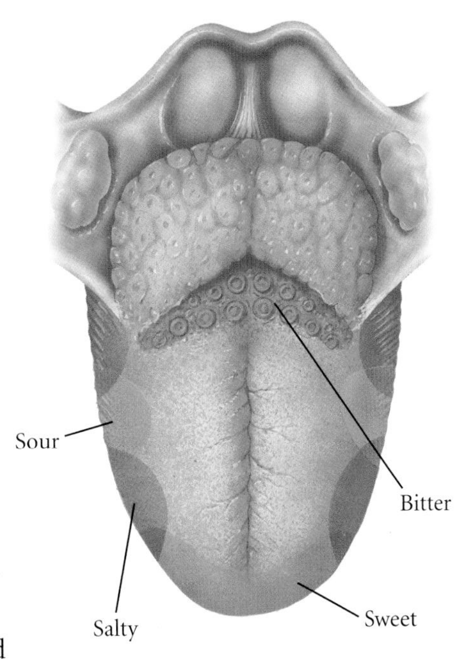

- **Taste buds** are receptor cells found around tiny bumps called papillae on the surface of your tongue.
- **Taste buds** are sensitive to four basic flavours: sweet, sour, bitter and salty.
- **The back of the tongue** contains big round papaillae shaped like an upside-down V. This is where bitter flavours are sensed.
- **The front of the tongue** is where fungiform (mushroom-like) papillae and filiform (hairlike) papillae carry taste buds that detect sweet, sour and salty flavours.
- **As well as taste,** the tongue can also feel the texture and temperature of food.
- **Your sense of taste** works closely together with your sense of smell to make the flavour of food more interesting.
- **Strong tastes,** such as spicy food, rely less on the sense of smell than on pain-sensitive nerve endings in the tongue.
- **People can learn** to distinguish more flavours and tastes than normal, as is the case with tea- or wine-tasters.

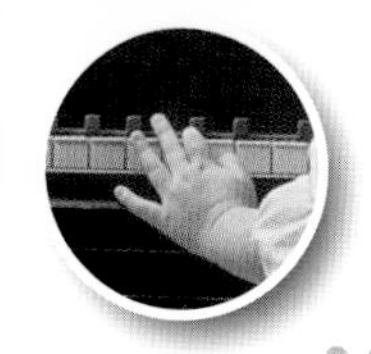

Touch

- **Touch,** or physical contact, is just one of the five sensations that are spread all over your body in your skin. The others indude pressure, pain, hot and cold.
- **There are sense receptors** everywhere in your skin, but places like your face have more than your back.
- **There are 200,000** hot and cold receptors in your skin, plus 500,000 touch and pressure receptors, and nearly 3 million pain receptors.
- **Free nerve-endings** are rather like the bare end of a wire. They respond to all five kinds of skin sensation and are almost everywhere in your skin.
- **There are specialized receptors** in certain places, each named after their discoverer.

▲ *The fingertips are where your sense of touch is most sensitive.*

...FASCINATING FACT...

Your brain knows just how hard you are touched from how fast nerve signals arrive.

▲ *As we grow up, we gradually learn to identify more and more things instantly through touch.*

- **Pacini's corpuscles** and Meissner's endings react instantly to sudden pressure.
- **Krause's bulbs**, Merkel's discs and Ruffini's endings respond to steady pressure.
- **Krause's bulbs** are also sensitive to cold.
- **Ruffini's endings** also react to changes in temperature.

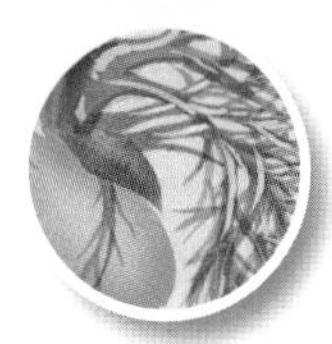

Index